The Drama Group

Hug ...se Library
... on Trust

and Nigel Hollins

illustrated by Lisa Kopper

D1100574

Beyond Words

London

Foreword

I often have a moan about acting as a job when I'm doing interviews. It's partly because film acting IS a bit slow and dull. And partly because I can't quite bring myself to spout the usual stuff about how wonderful the experience of making whatever film it was has been, and how much acting heals my spirit, etc, etc.

BUT, I will say this. Amateur acting was always a genuine pleasure. I had a real laugh doing plays at school and university. I genuinely loved the performing, the excitement, the bonding, the romances with the girl playing Masha, the cast parties, the backbiting, everything. It's an experience that I do heartily recommend to anyone who's curious and hasn't yet tried it.

That's one of the reasons I was keen to lend a hand in the making of this book. The other was my admiration for this series of books as a whole. I hadn't come across them until my friends Sheila and Nigel Hollins introduced me to them and I thought they were genius. The three of us, together with some other friends, sat around and came up with the story that follows. And then the brilliant Lisa Kopper did the drawings. I hope people like the finished thing. I'm very proud of it.

Hugh Grant

Contents

41

Storyline

The following words are provided for readers and supporters who want some ideas about one possible story. Most readers make their own story up from the pictures.

1. Dean goes to the theatre with his family.

2. Dad buys tickets and a programme for the show.

3. Dean watches the show. He's happy.

4. The show ends and everyone claps. Dean cheers loudly.

5. He asks one of the stars for an autograph.

6. Dean and his family go home on the bus. They talk about the show all the way home.

7. Dean and James meet in a café. They look at the programme for the show.

8. James asks Dean, "Do you want to act?" He shows him a book about acting.

9. Dean goes to visit a drama club with James. He's nervous.

10. It's the tea break. Everyone looks at Dean. He doesn't know any of them.

11. Dean meets the drama tutor, Carol. Scary!

12. Carol introduces him, "Let's welcome Dean."

13. Carol says, "We've got a new activity today. Listen carefully and join in."

48

14. Carol takes a card out of a hat. The card has a picture of an angry face on it. She shows it to Ronnie.

15. Ronnie pretends to be angry, like the picture. Everyone watches him. They have to guess what emotion he's acting.

16. Ronnie takes a card with a surprised face on it, and shows it to Jacky.

17. Jacky acts surprised, like the picture. Everyone watches carefully. Dean thinks, "Wow!"

18. Jacky takes a card with a happy face on it, and shows it to Dean. He's really scared.

19. Dean runs to the toilet – he thinks he can't do it.

20. James knocks on the door. "Are you alright?" Dean won't come out.

21. James and Dean come back to the group. Carol says, "Welcome back. Don't be shy."

22. Now they all work in pairs. They have some props. Dean is with Jacky. He joins in and looks happy.

23. Dean and Jacky dress up as different characters. They have fun together.

24. Later, the group gets ready to rehearse a play. Carol talks them through the story.

25. Carol talks to the group about each character. She points at Jacky, "Do you want to be Juliet?" Jacky says, "Yes please!"

26. Carol points at the picture of Romeo and asks Ronnie to play Romeo. He says, "Thank you. I'm thrilled!"

27. Carol asks Dean to play a part. He says, "No way!"

28. Carol gives Dean a paintbrush. She says, "You can paint the scenery instead of acting." Dean is happy to do the painting.

29. Dean paints the scenery and watches Jacky and Ronnie rehearse for the play. He really wants to take part!

30. Dean watches the sword fight. Ronnie and Simon practise their fight.

31. Dean has a go at sword fighting. Jacky watches from behind the curtain.

32. Jacky says to Dean, "You're good at this part."

33. Dean watches the rehearsals of Romeo and Juliet from backstage.

34. Ronnie climbs up to Jacky on the balcony. Dean and Carol are worried. Carol says, "Stop – that's dangerous!"

35. Ronnie falls down. "Aaaaah!"

36. The paramedic looks at Ronnie's arm. He says, "I think your arm is broken."

37. The paramedic takes Ronnie to the hospital. Carol asks Dean to play Romeo.

38. The audience arrives for the play Romeo and Juliet.

39. Jacky and Dean are backstage with Carol. They get ready to go on stage. Dean's very nervous.

40. Dean's on the stage. He's in the spotlight. Dean says his first lines as Romeo.

41. Dean climbs up the ladder to Juliet. It's a love scene. He feels confident and happy.

42. Dean enjoys fighting on stage with Simon. It's fun.

43. They bow at the end of the play. The audience clap and take photos. Dean's family cheer him.

44. Dean and Jacky are happy. The play was a great success.

45. Everyone queues up for Dean's autograph at the stage door. Dean's sister says, "You're the star of the show."

46. Dean and Jacky go on a date to see a show.

Acting

Why do people start acting?

People start acting for many reasons. So what about you? It could be that you want to make friends, do something fun, or grow in confidence. You may have dreams of becoming famous one day or simply want to perform in a play on a real stage. Perhaps someone has recommended joining a drama group, or like Dean, you may have been inspired by some actors on stage or screen.

Different kinds of acting

There are many different kinds of acting and drama styles. From comedy and improvisations to melodrama or Shakespeare, you're sure to find something which suits you. Many drama groups will explore a range of acting styles depending on the play. Sometimes you will be trying to make everything realistic, drawing on your own life experiences, but then at other times you may just have to use your imagination.

The importance of backstage roles

Drama groups need lots of different kinds of people, not just budding actors. A play couldn't go on without the lights, props, costumes, music or direction.

Directors and assistant directors pull the whole show together, running the rehearsals and making important decisions. Technicians operate light and sound, set designers build the stage and make-up artists make actors look their best. They can age or disguise them too. Stage managers like Dean are crucial for finding and organising props and making sure actors know what's happening off stage, and they often need an assistant. These roles are just the tip of the iceberg; there are many other people that help to pull a show together: costume designers, stage hands, artists and ushers, to name a few.

The importance of commitment

All of the behind-the-scenes 'magic' actually takes a lot of hard work and preparation for everyone involved. Rehearsals are not just important for the cast, the crew need to understand the needs of the play too. Putting on a play is a commitment and people rely on you to turn up on time, ready to work. If you don't, you let the whole group down, so it's a big responsibility.

It is a good idea to create a contract with the group at the beginning of rehearsals, where everyone shares thoughts on how to behave, and promises to commit to the project. This especially includes no holidays or having a day off during the performance week, otherwise the show can't go on – *everyone* is needed.

Falling in love: on stage and in real life

Love for everyone is an extremely complex emotion. When reciprocated it has the power to completely change your life for the better, but if unrequited it can leave your feelings in tatters.

It can be hard for anyone to keep feelings of 'love' acted on stage separate from feelings experienced in reality, and the same is true for someone with a learning disability. No one should be discouraged from acting romantically on stage. But it is the responsibility of facilitators to help actors to separate their characters and fantasy from reality.

- Be very clear about who you are referring to when addressing actors.

  Whilst a person is acting on stage you could refer to them using their character's name, for example "Juliet, now you move to the balcony."

  As soon as you're off stage or breaking out of acting to discuss personal thoughts, use the actor's real name, for example "OK let's break there. Well done, Claire. I think you're really getting the hang of how Juliet is thinking."

- De-role after each session: say goodbye to the character, shaking them off, and say hello to the real you.

- Encourage actors to shake hands with each other and talk about how good the rehearsal was; this helps reduce any character tensions transferring over to real life.

- Where possible, when discussing characters, use a visual stimulus to clarify things. For example, you could use this book to show how Dean is the real person, an 'actor', and Romeo is the pretend person, his 'character'.

Building confidence, making friends

Drama and theatre have long been known to boost confidence and build self-esteem. They have an amazing power to help those who have difficulties in social contexts to relate to one another, providing a platform on which friendships and bonds are formed.

Through the use of theatre games and warm ups, we learn to be more comfortable and trusting of those around us, sharing in the special experiences which occur in the safety net of our drama group.

Ice-breakers are a wonderful way to begin a drama session, getting us used to each other. For example they can encourage eye contact which someone might find too daunting in another context, thus paving the way for the 'real' acting or role plays to occur.

Books Beyond Words role play

You can use this book as a visual stimulus for setting up role plays, to help think about emotions and for ideas of warm-up games.

When exploring emotions with the group you could choose a single page from the book or a few continuing pages for actors to study. Discuss in the context of the story how they think a character may be feeling. For instance in pictures 10, 13, 18 and 39, Dean might be feeling nervous.

Role play some scenes from the book with someone playing Dean and someone playing the other characters, for example picture 20, where Dean's support worker is talking to Dean through the toilet door.

You could use questions such as:

- What is he saying to Dean?

- What is Dean saying?

- How does he get Dean to go back to the group?

Watch some of the role plays as a group. You could choose some other scenes from the book to role play in the same way. Remember to get your actors to shake hands after a scene, particularly if there's been an argument or fight, or a love scene.

End the session by saying goodbye to the characters and closing the book. Put any props back in their box. Shake hands with the members of the group. You may like to finish with a game again, or a discussion about what they enjoyed and would like to do next time. Other books in the Books Beyond Words series also provide a resource for role plays.

For groups who are interested in putting on a full production of *The Drama Group*, a complete script, developed for performance by the Baked Bean Theatre Company, is included in the *Beyond Words Drama Handbook* (see page 59).

Dramatherapy

What is dramatherapy?

Dramatherapy is an expressive form of psychotherapy which uses creative media to explore feelings and issues. It is the intentional use of healing aspects of drama and theatre as part of a therapeutic process. The tools that are used can range from drama and projection right the way through to the use of script and performance. Examples of the range of artistic interventions a dramatherapist may employ include improvised drama, text, stories, myths, puppetry, masks, voice and play, and sometimes also aspects of movement, art and music. These methods facilitate creativity, imagination, learning, insight and growth.

Dramatherapists are both artists and clinicians and draw on their trainings in theatre/drama and therapy to engage the people they work with and bring about psychological, emotional and social changes. The therapy gives equal value to body and mind within the dramatic context. These methods can enable the client to explore difficult and painful life experiences often through an indirect approach.

Dramatherapists help their clients to find the best medium for them to engage in, whether as part of a group or in individual therapy to address and resolve, or make troubling issues more bearable. Dramatherapy is an evidence-based approach and one of the four recognised and accredited creative arts psychotherapies (drama, dance and movement, art, and music). In the UK, dramatherapists are required to complete recognised professional training at masters degree level in order to work, as well as registration with the Health and Care Professions Council (HCPC). Only those who fulfil these criteria can use the title dramatherapist.

Dramatherapists work in a wide variety of settings, including schools, mental health services, social care settings, prisons and their own private practices.

The people they work with have differing needs: from children on the autistic spectrum to older people with dementia; adolescents who self-harm; people with histories of sexual and/or physical abuse; those suffering from a mental illness; people with learning disabilities and women with post-natal depression.

Someone seeing a dramatherapist needs no previous experience or interest in performing arts or drama. All the work is confidential, as with any form of psychotherapy or counselling.

How can you find a local dramatherapist?

The best way to find a dramatherapist in your local area, who is properly trained and registered, is through the British Association of Dramatherapists (BADth): www.badth.org.uk

You can check their registration details with the Health and Care Professions Council: www.hcpc-uk.org.uk/aboutus

Useful resources

Beyond Words Drama Handbook by Jade Hardrade-Grosz and James Wheildon (Books Beyond Words, 2014)
A guide for anyone looking to start up or find new ideas for a drama group for people with learning disabilities. It shows how to set up sessions, and how to plan and facilitate a variety of pieces of drama, using Books Beyond Words stories as a point of inspiration.
www.booksbeyondwords.co.uk/bookshop/paperbacks/beyond-words-drama-handbook

Special Talents, Special Needs: Drama for People with Learning Disabilities by Ian McCurrach and Barbara Darnley (Jessica Kingsley, 1999)
A handbook for teachers and facilitators working with people interested in creative expression through drama, this text provides a step-by-step guide to running a drama group.

Groupwork with Learning Disabilities: Creative Drama by Anna Chesner (Speechmark, 1998)
This practical manual is aimed at anyone facilitating creative drama. It demonstrates how drama can deliver many benefits to both individuals and groups, including increased tolerance and respect, enhancing self-esteem and developing social skills. It includes many easy-to-follow exercises and activities.

101 Drama Games and Activities by David Farmer (Lulu, 2011)
101 games and exercises suitable for use in drama lessons, workshops or rehearsals with children, young people or adults. Chapters include improvisation, mime, ice-breakers, group dynamics, rehearsal, story-telling, voice and warm ups.

Dramatherapy for People with Learning Disabilities: A World of Difference by Anna Chesner (Jessica Kingsley, 1994)
This book explores the value of action-based therapy methods with people with learning disabilities, both in terms of theory and practice. Using case history examples of technique, the author considers the multidisciplinary potentials of dramatherapy, and explores collaborations with speech therapy and music therapy.

Introduction to Dramatherapy: Theatre and Healing – Ariadne's Ball of Thread by Sue Jennings (Jessica Kingsley, 1997)
This book presents a 'healing theatre' approach to dramatherapy.The book also includes exercises and questionnaires which can be used with students.

Developmental Drama: Dramatherapy Approaches for People with Profound or Severe Multiple Disabilities, Including Sensory Impairment by Mary Booker (Jessica Kingsley, 2011)
This is an accessible guide for practitioners looking to use drama in work with people with severe or profound multiple disabilities (PMLD), but are unsure where to begin.

Online resources

We have included additional information on our website, including a list of drama groups for people with learning disabilities throughout the UK:
www.booksbeyondwords.co.uk/bookshop/paperbacks/drama-group

Related titles in the Books Beyond Words series

Falling in Love (1999) by Sheila Hollins, Wendy Perez and Adam Abdelnoor, illustrated by Beth Webb. This love story follows the relationship between Mike and Janet from their first date through to deciding to become engaged to be married.

Speaking Up for Myself (2002) by Sheila Hollins, Jackie Downer, Linette Farquarson and Oyepeju Raji, illustrated by Lisa Kopper. Having a learning disability and being from an ethnic minority group can make it hard to get good services. Natalie learns to fix problems by being assertive and getting help from someone she trusts.

Michelle Finds a Voice (1997) by Sheila Hollins and Sarah Barnett, illustrated by Denise Redmond. Michelle cannot speak and is unable to communicate her thoughts and feelings. She feels isolated and unhappy. Michelle and the people who support her try signing, symbols and electronic aids to find a solution that works.

George Gets Smart (2003) by Sheila Hollins, Margaret Flynn and Philippa Russell, illustrated by Catherine Brighton. George's life changes when he learns how to keep clean and smart. People no longer avoid being with him and he enjoys the company of his friends.

Enjoying Sport and Exercise (2008) by Sheila Hollins and Caroline Argent, illustrated by Catherine Brighton. Jasmine is a wheelchair user who takes up badminton while her mum does Tai Chi; Charlie, who is overweight, discovers dog walking and cricket; James is a runner who fulfils his ambition to run a marathon.

Authors and artist

Hugh Grant, film actor and campaigner, advocate and friend to people with learning disabilities, shares his love of acting with a new audience.

Sheila Hollins, founder and editor of the Books Beyond Words series, psychiatrist and independent member of the House of Lords, seeks to encourage full participation and inclusion in the creative and performing arts.

Nigel Hollins, the original inspiration for Books Beyond Words and advisor to many titles, is also an amateur actor and recently appeared (very briefly!) as an extra in Hugh Grant's 'The Rewrite'.

Lisa Kopper is a distinguished artist and illustrator of children's books. She is well-known for her clear style and ability to draw feelings as well as form. Lisa is artist in residence at Acton Court: www.actoncourt.com

Acknowledgments

We thank our editorial advisors Kate Powell, Suzanne Cutler and Gus Lewandowski, for their ideas and advice about what was needed in the pictures.

Many thanks to all the people who supported individuals and groups to trial the pictures: Sue Carmichael, Book Club Co-ordinator (supported by Steve Chapman, the Dover discovery book club; Wendy Satherly, Sittingbourne Pulse Café book club; Andrew Skelt, Dartford Monday book club; and Denise Fielding, Thurrock book club); Viv Colvill and the Freewheelers Theatre Company, Leatherhead (supported by Liz Tye, Pip Steers, Andrew Marber, Luke Hinsley and Sonas Musana); Jean-Christophe Larkin and Perseid Upper School, Morden; and Chloe Moffat from the Baked Bean Theatre Company, Wandsworth (supported by Maureen Davey and Ivor Potter).

We are grateful for the advice and support of our advisory group, which included Noëlle Blackman, dramatherapist and CEO of Respond, Jade Hardrade-Grosz, Director, and Chloe Moffat, drama teacher, from the Baked Bean Theatre Company, for the time they gave most generously and the experience they shared with us, and for their assistance with the text.

Finally, we are very grateful to Hugh Grant for his inspiration, commitment and generous financial support for this book.

Beyond Words: publications and training

Books Beyond Words will also help family carers, support workers and professionals working with people who find pictures easier than words for understanding their world. A list of all Beyond Words publications, including Books Beyond Words titles, and where to buy them, can be found on our website:

www.booksbeyondwords.co.uk

Workshops about using Books Beyond Words are provided regularly in London, or can be arranged in other localities on request. Self-advocates are welcome. For information about forthcoming workshops see our website or contact us:

Email: admin@booksbeyondwords.co.uk

Tel: 020 8725 5512

Video clips showing our books being read are also on our website and YouTube channel: www.youtube.com/user/booksbeyondwords and on our DVD, *How to Use Books Beyond Words*.